Photo Credit:
Artwork by Sawsan El-Gamal, "Relationship"

Copyright © 2019 Ali Hussain
All rights reserved.
ISBN: 9781701935822

دائمًا في سبيل الواحد الأحد، الذي هو حقيقة كل مرائي الشكر

وإلى المرآة الكاملة وأصل الحمد والجمال، محمد ﷺ

وإلى سلطان الأولياء وغوث قلبي، مولانا الشيخ ناظم. أخذتني من صحراء الصور إلى حوراء الحقائق السماوية

وإلى قطبي المتصرف المحمدي، مولانا الشيخ محمد هشام قباني. في حضرتك، أنا مع قمر بني هاشم.

وإلى أمهاتي الروحيتين، الحجة آمنة والحجة نزيهة. أمانتكم ونزاهتكم يغمروننا بصفاء الزهراء.

وإلى والدي زهير وسوسن، أنتما ريحانتي قلبي والجناحين الذين أطير بهما.

وإلى فاطمتي وزهرتي. معكما، أنا أكتمل.

الفن في ذكريات: شد الرحال
Art in Memoirs: Setting Forth

Always for the sake of the Almighty One, Who is The Reality of All Mirrors of Gratitude.

And to that Perfect Mirror, the principle of praise and beauty, Muhammad.

And to the Sultan of Saints and my heart's succor, Mawlana Shaykh Nazim. You took me from the desert of forms to the dessert of heavenly norms.

And to my Muhammadan Pole of Power and Grace, Mawlana Shaykh Hisham. In your presence, I'm with the Hashemite King.

And to my spiritual mothers, Hajjah Amina and Hajjah Naziha, your Amana and Nazaha engulf us in the purity of al-Zahra.

And to my parents, Zohair and Sawsan, you are the roses of my heart and wings with which I fly.

And to my Fatima and Zahra,
With you I'm complete.

الفن في ذكريات: شد الرحال
Art in Memoirs: Setting Forth

الفهرست

المقدمة	XIV
لقاء المواسم	18
من الفنان إلى الفن	20
شلال العشق	22
حصن القهوة المتواضعة	24
الولاية في سن كبير	26
إعتاق الماضي	28
عرض لطيف	30
عندما يتكلم العود	32
بحري الفنان	34
الخلاص في الكتب؟ كلا، في البحر!	36
بين الخوف والطمع	38
من نسمات النور إلى الصور	40
نسائم العشق	42
مسكن الفن والذكريات	44
شكر. إعتاق. فن	46
حياة الفنانين القاتلة	48

الفن في ذكريات: شد الرحال
Art in Memoirs: Setting Forth

على أعتاب البرزخ	50
على ساحل التعبير	52
تلاميذ الفرشة والصوت	54
جاذبية الفن	56
الموسيقى وخديعة البحار	58
الصدفة والعجب	60
في يدي حرفتك	62
فن الفراق	64
مسكن الفن	66
في عمق العاصفة	68
عطش الموسيقى	70
شغف الفنان	72
الأصالة بين الأوتار	74
شعور الفنان الأزلي	76
من التيهور إلى الانضباط	78
بين العناق والافتراق	80
على خطى الأولياء	82
همسات الصوت	84
قناع شهوات الروح	86

لوحة فارغة وريشة غامضة	88
الشعور بجمال الضنك	90
جوهرة تتصبب عرقا	92
يا حضرة الفنان	94
استفسار فني	96
تشدق نغمات الإبداع	98
لا تغادر أرض الفن	100
حوار السوق	102
مسكن العقل والمنطق	104
لغة أقدم من الزمن	106
غذاء من الفراق	108

الفن في ذكريات: شد الرحال
Art in Memoirs: Setting Forth

Contents

Preface	xv
The Meeting of Seasons	19
From Artist to Art	21
The Waterfall of Love	23
The Fortress of Humble Coffee	25
Sainthood at Old Age	27
The Past's Liberation	29
A Subtle Spectacle	31
When the Oud Speaks	33
The Artist's Two Oceans	35
A Refuge in Books? Nay, Oceans!	37
Between Hope and Fear	39
From Auras of Light to Forms	41
The Zephyrs of Amor	43
The House of Art and Memories	45
Gratitude. Redemption. Art	47
The Deadly Life of Artists	49
At the Interstice	51
At the Shore of Expression	53
Students of Brush and Sound	55
The Artist's Attraction	57
Music and Deceitful Oceans	59
Serendipity and Wonder	61
In the Hands of Your Craft	63
The Art of Letting Go	65

الفن في ذكريات: شد الرحال
Art in Memoirs: Setting Forth

Where Art Resides	67
In the Eye of the Storm	69
The Thirst of Music	71
The Desire of the Artist	73
Heritage Between The Strings	75
The Artist's Immortal Feelings	77
From the Avalanche to Order	79
Between Embraces and Separation	81
Upon the Footsteps of Saints	83
The Whispers of Sound	85
The Mask of The Spirit's Desire	87
An Empty Canvas, Unknown Brush	89
Sensing the Beauty of Misery	91
The Prespirating Jewel	93
Dear Mr. Artist	95
An Artistic Inquiry	97
Melodies of Declamation	99
Don't Depart from the Land of Art	101
A Conversation at the Marketplace	103
The Abode of Intellect and Logic	105
A Language Older Than Time	107
The Sustenance of Separation	109

المقدمة

ما هو دور اللغة في التعبير عن الإلهام الفني والحالة الإبداعية؟ هل يستطيع كلام البشر أن يومئ بحروف محدودة وكلمات مسجونة وجمل ضيقة عن جنون الفنان وهو يعيش في مكانة خارج حيز المكان وفي وقت بعيد عن إطار الدهر؟

هذا الكتاب يحوي أكثر من أربعين تأملا شعريا في صورة نثر على هوجاء الفن حين يطيح بعقل الفنان. وتشمل هذه الرقصات القصيرة على قطع تشيد بقبائل جميع الفنون من كتابة ورسم ونحت وعزف على الأوتار.

كتبت هذه التأملات وغيرها في نهاية عام 2018. جميع ما تقرأ هنا أخي العزيز كانت بدايته استماع ونهايته إنصات، لا غير. قد يأتي الإلهام مرة على صورة فكرة ومرة على فكرة في صورة الصوت وتناغم الحروف. فما على الكاتب حينئذ سوى نقل المعنى في صور حتى نهاية المطاف.

الفن في ذكريات: شد الرحال
Art in Memoirs: Setting Forth

PREFACE

What is the role of language in expressing what artistic inspiration and the creative state? Can human speech even allude with limited letters, imprisoned words and narrow sentences to the insanity of the artist whilst they reside in a space outside of place and in a moment distant from time?

This book contains more than 40 poetic reflections in the form of prose, all revolving around the madness of art when it overthrows the reason of the artist. These short dances include movements that pay homage to the tribes of all art forms, including writing, painting, sculpting and music.

These reflections and others were written at the end of 2018. All that you read here, my dear friend, began and ended with attentive listening. Inspiration might come in the form of an idea, while another instance in the idea of the form of sound and harmony of letters. Then, the writer can only transmit the meaning until the end.

الفن في ذكريات: شد الرحال
Art in Memoirs: Setting Forth

لقاء المواسم

عندما يلتقي الربيع مع الخريف، تبدأ الأوراق الساقطة فجأة بأداء معزوفة صفاء الحياة في مسيرة من سماء الخضار نزولا إلى صحراء الفناء.

الفن في ذكريات: شد الرحال
Art in Memoirs: Setting Forth

THE MEETING OF SEASONS

When Spring meets Autumn, suddenly the falling leaves perform a symphony of pure life in their march from the heavens of greenery towards the desert of annihilation.

من الفنان إلى الفن

الرسام، الموسيقي، الممثل أو الشاعر يبدأ رحلته في صورة خاصة من الفن ولكن عليه أن يتعدى عاجلا أم آجلا حدود فنه ليصل إلى ساحل الفن بكليته. هذا لا يعني أن الفنان عليه أن يحتضن جميع أنواع الفن ظاهرا، ولكن عليه أن يُجَسِّد منبع الإبداع الذي تفيض منه جميع بحور الفن.

الفنان الذي استطاع أن يصل إلى هذه المرتبة قد يتحرر أيضا من حسن التجسد ليصبح معزوفة الفن بحد ذاتها، تدوي آثارها في أثير اللازمن. عندما تقابل شبح إبداعي كهذا، تجد أن كل سلوك يصطنعه الفنان يأخذك إلى ماض في عصر سحيق. هنالك قد ترى وتسمع في شخص مثل هذا الفنان أنواع الفنون في سكونهم وفكرهم قبل حركاتهم وأنفاسهم.

الفن في ذكريات: شد الرحال
Art in Memoirs: Setting Forth

FROM ARTIST TO ART

The painter, musician, actor or poet begin their journey in a specific form but must eventually transcend the bounds of this physical craft to arrive at the shore of all art.

This does not mean that the artist embraces all these art forms outwardly, but rather embodies inwardly the well of creativity from which all these oceans flow.

Such an artist may even escape the prison of embodiment and become a symphony of art itself, playing in the ether of timelessness.

When you encounter such a creative apparition, their every mannerism takes you back to an epoch immemorial. You hear and see artwork in their very stillness.

شلال العشق

عندما تكون عاشقا، تبدأ تشاهد كل الجمال وكأنه شلالا يتراقص في طريقه إلى السكون في قلب المعشوق. وبعدها، يقوم مرة ثانية في نور، في مولد جديد يصبح فيه قصيدة لا تنتهي، تمطر قطرات من الرؤى الوجدية آتية من سماء الإبداع الإلهي.

الفن في ذكريات: شد الرحال
Art in Memoirs: Setting Forth

THE WATERFALL OF LOVE

When you are in love, you begin to witness all of beauty as a waterfall that dances its way to stillness in the heart of your beloved. And then, it rises again in light, reborn as an endless poem that rains down in captivating visions from the heavens of divine creativity.

حصن القهوة المتواضعة

هنالك أيام ترغب لو انك تُحَصّن فيها جميع وجدانك داخل فنجان من القهوة.

تتمنى لو تسمح لأريجها بأن يلبس بصرك زيا من الكشف كي تشاهد تاريخ كل شيء، ليس مكتوبا في سجلات من الأساطير، ولكن أداء ملموسا يتكون من ألوان زائلة و أسطح فائتة.

إن القهوة هي نفسها الحالة الإبداعية ولكن في زي آخر. فهي تحيي كل شيء، حتى الموت، لكي يقوموا بسرد قصة واحدة لا غير.

الفن في ذكريات: شد الرحال
Art in Memoirs: Setting Forth

THE FORTRESS OF HUMBLE COFFEE

There are days when you desire to fortify your entire being with a humble cup of coffee.

You wish to allow its aroma to dress your sight with the unveiling necessary to witness the history of all things, not in written genealogies, but a textured performance of withered colors and faded surfaces.

Coffee is the creative state in disguise. It brings all things, even death, to life in order to narrate but a single story.

الولاية في سن كبير

الولاية هي القدرة على التعبير في سكون لا تستطيع الكلمة المكتوبة أن تمحي عنه ستار الظلمة إلا في سن هرم.

فإذا كانت الكلمة المكتوبة هي البحر، فالولاية هي الماء الذي تحرر من سجن الاجساد.

الفن في ذكريات: شد الرحال
Art in Memoirs: Setting Forth

SAINTHOOD AT OLD AGE

Sainthood is to express in stillness what the written word can only illuminate at old age.

If the written word is the ocean, then sainthood is water liberated from the prison of bodies.

إعتاق الماضي

لا تتجاهل حركات الأماكن من ماضيك وهي تحرر أنفسها في الأحلام والخيال من سجن الصور.

ولا تستخف بالعلاقات الغريبة التي تفرض نفسها في نسيج ذاكرتك والتي تخون نواميس العالم الملموس.

ربما هذه هي الطريقة التي تعلمك من خلالها الروح أنها هي المتحكمة بزمام الأمور. وربما هذه هي الوسيلة التي من خلالها تستطيع المعاني أن تحرك الملموسات.

بل ربما عالمنا المشهود هذا بتفرقته وتنازعاته ما هو إلا مجموعة أدلة تشهد على وحدة متجانسة ومخفية تكمن خلف ستار من البصيرة المبهمة من شدة النور.

الفن في ذكريات: شد الرحال
Art in Memoirs: Setting Forth

THE PAST'S LIBERATION

Do not dismiss the way places from your past liberate themselves from the prison of forms in your dreams and imagination.

Do not belittle the infringing foreign connections between textures in your memory that betray the canons of the physical world.

Perhaps this is the way that the spirit lets you know it is in control. Perhaps this is how metaphysics animates physics.

Perhaps the dispersed and disconnected nature of our visible world is merely a clue of a connected unity, hidden behind a blinding and dazzling in-visibility.

عرض لطيف

اعلم أن هنالك نفسا وحيدة أخرى قريبة منك تشعر بطوفان المشاعر الذي يسري عندما يتحدث لسان يدك بالموسيقى، تلك النفس هي آلتك الموسيقية.

آلتك لديها منبع من هذه الابتهالات خامد في عمق فراغها. مع كل وتر ينبض فيها، روحها أيضا تضحي بقطعة من ذاتها إليك وفي سبيلك. هذا الجزء من السلام يصل إليك في صورة زفير من رائحة الخشب العتيق.

أحضر نفسك قريبا وزد معانقتك قوة يا صديقي، حتى تستطيع أن تشاهد هذا العرض اللطيف.

الفن في ذكريات: شد الرحال
Art in Memoirs: Setting Forth

A SUBTLE SPECTACLE

Know that the only other soul in close proximity to you that feels the tidal wave of emotions flowing through when the tongue of your hand speaks through music is your instrument.

Your instrument has a spring of these invocations lingering deep in its emptiness. With each vibration, its spirit sacrifices a piece of its own self for your sake. This peace reaches you in the form of an ancient wooden breeze.

Bring yourself closer and tighten your embrace in order to witness this subtle spectacle my friend.

عندما يتكلم العود

يحاورني العود مرة أخرى: "لا يمكن لنا أن نتحدث سويا حتى تكرس نفسك لهذا الصوت!" فاستمعت وما زلت أنصت، حتى أنني بدأت اسمع ضواحي كل نوتة وكأنها بحر من الأصوات.

كل نوتة تصقل نغمة إيقاع قلبي لكي تنسجم مع سيرتها الذاتية الخاصة بها. وبعد ذلك، يظهر المنبع الإلهي لكي يندمج مرة أخرى في شهود حقيقة أن كل جملة موسيقية ما هي إلا ملحمة عريقة بحد ذاتها.

الفن في ذكريات: شد الرحال
Art in Memoirs: Setting Forth

WHEN THE OUD SPEAKS

The Oud speaks to me again: "We cannot converse until you devote yourself to this sound!".
So I listened, and I continue to hearken, until I began to hear the contours of every note as an ocean of sounds.

Every note tones the tune of my heart's rhythm to its distinct story. The divine origin of this journey then emerges and merges once again to testify that every musical sentence is an ancient epic by itself.

بحري الفنان

ذات كل فنان تتطلع للإرتواء من بحرين، كلاهما ينبع من قطرة واحدة من الابداع.

وقلب الفنان يتشغف لشرب هذين البحرين كاملا من أكواب الفن. فبينما هو يروي عطشه، يتراقص البحرين في وجدانه ويتفوهان بأسرار لا تعرفها اللغة.

خلال هذا الأداء، يجلس الفنان ويستمع، يكتشف نفسه وذاته من خلال الصمت ومشاهدة سره وهو يتجلى من خلال فيضان شهواته وتطلعاته.

الفن في ذكريات: شد الرحال

Art in Memoirs: Setting Forth

THE ARTIST'S TWO OCEANS

The soul of every artist craves to drink from two oceans, both of which spring from a single drop of creativity.

The heart of the artist craves to drink these two oceans in their entirety through the cups of their crafts. As they quench their thirst, the oceans whirl within their conscience and communicate secrets unknown to language itself.

Meanwhile, the artist sits and listens, discovering himself in the process of silence and witnessing his secret in the unfolding of desires.

الخلاص في الكتب؟ كلا، في البحر!

أي مأوى تأمل أن تجد في كتبك؟ هل تبحث عن ملجأ بين أحضان الحبر العتيق الذي لا يتجاوز حدود صورة جامدة مكونة من كلمات تجسد تاريخ ذاكرة محتضرة؟

البعض يبحث عن نوع من الاستقرار بين أحضان هياكل المعاني الموسومة للإنتقام من قهر طوفان المشاعر الذي يحملهم بعيدا عن جلال البحر.

ولكن كما أن ازدهار الطبيعة يومئ إلى نزاهة الخضار في سماء الألوان، فأنا وأنت يا صديقي نحتاج أن نتجاوز أمواج الكلمات إلى شاطئ المشاهدة والذوق. ليس شاطئ البحر وحسب، بل الماء بجد ذاته وهو في حرية كاملة!

الفن في ذكريات: شد الرحال
Art in Memoirs: Setting Forth

A REFUGE IN BOOKS? NAY, OCEANS!

What refuge do you hope to find in your books? Are you seeking a shelter within the confines of ancient ink that is nothing more than a frozen image in words of a passing memory?

Some are seeking stability amidst these imprinted effigies of meaning to compensate for the tidal waves of emotion carrying them away from the immensity of oceans.

But just as the glory of nature beckons towards the transcendence of greenery in the heaven of colors, you and I my friend are in need of transcending the waves of words to witness and taste, not only the ocean, but water itself in its complete liberation!

بين الخوف و الطمع

عندما يشعر الفنان بالاكتئاب، فإنه بسبب التداعيات التي تحمله بعيدا، ولو لفترة قليلة، عن مصدر إلهامه.

السعادة قد لا تأتي إلى الفنان عندما ينتج عملا فنيا ظاهرا، ولكن عندما يرى نفسه في حضور دائم داخل الحالة الابداعية وفي تذوقه الدائم للرونق الذي يضيفه الفن كزي فوق صور الكون.

كفنانين، يجب علينا أن نستمع إلى أعمق الأصوات التي تُسَيّر اهتمامنا وأنظارنا نحو آثار المشاعر التي تعانق أرواحنا والتي تدعونا دائمًا نحو المجهول.

الفن في ذكريات: شد الرحال
Art in Memoirs: Setting Forth

BETWEEN HOPE AND FEAR

Whenever an artist feels depressed, it is because distractions have moved them ever so slightly away from their incessant channel of inspiration.

Happiness does not come to the artist because they produce art outwardly, but when they see themselves in constant presence in the creative state and their indelible taste of the enchantment which art places as a dress upon the forms of the universe.

As artists, we must listen to the deepest of voices directing our attention to the emotional traces married to our spirits and which constantly call us to the unknown.

من نسمات النور إلى الصور

يولد الفن في ومضات من النور ترقد خلف أفق الصورة والجسد. ويظهر الفن في عالم الصورة في تجليات مبهمة من الجمال تلبي رغبات الحواس الست كلها.

داخل هذه الومضات تكمن قمم جبال الكمال التي تلمس بشوقها قبب خضار السماء. هذا الشوق ما هو إلا مهرجان أزلي يشهده كل من يقصد تلك الأنغام التي تُعزف في تلك القمم.

هؤلاء المريدون يُعطَون مثل هذا الذوق لكي يعلموا أن حتى قمم الازدهار لديها شوق يفوق الكلمات. فبعد مولد الفن الأول، لا يوجد إلا شوق يتجلى بلحظات رقيقة من العناق.

الفن في ذكريات: شد الرحال
Art in Memoirs: Setting Forth

FROM AURAS OF LIGHT TO FORMS

Art is born in figments of light beyond form and imagery. It emerges into the world of form in transcendent auras of beauty that accommodate the desires of all six senses.

Within these figments reside the mountain peaks of perfection that touch with their longing the domes of heavenly greenery. This is a timeless spectacle witnessed by all who seek the summit's symphony.

They are given such a vision in order to know that even these peaks of glory have a longing beyond words. After that initial birth of art, there is only longing made sweet by ephemeral moments of embrace.

نسائم العشق

تكاد تشتم نسيم الأحاديث بين الألوان من بعد، ولكن فقط إذا كانت هذه الألوان قد قُدّر لها الحب من قِبَل نظرات شاهدة.

العشق طاقة رابطة تُبعَثُ من شخصيات الألوان المختلفة و تعكس أسرارا في مرائيها الباطنة.

تأكد أن مثل هذه الألوان التي جُمعت سويا في الغربة تتكلم مع بعضها البعض وتُصدر أنفاسها ومضة تساوي رائحة تحمل بين أحضانها الذاكرة في كم هائل كالبحر.

الفن في ذكريات: شد الرحال
Art in Memoirs: Setting Forth

THE ZEPHYRS OF AMOR

You can almost smell the zephyr of conversations between colors from a distance, only if these hues have been destined for love by witnessing gazes.

Amor is a cohesive energy emerging from the distinctive tones of tints that refract secrets in their inner mirrors.

Rest assured, when colors such as these, that have been brought together in diaspora, speak with one another their breaths release a blink worth of a smell, carrying with it memory as an ocean.

مسكن الفن والذكريات

الذكريات تعيش علاقة حميمة مع الفن. فكلاهما يغذي الآخر بطرق رقيقة قد حُجبت سرا.

فدعني أرسم لك صورة المنزل الذي يعيش فيه هذين الزوجين، الفن والذكريات، منذ ولادة الزمن.

تخيل طريقا قد التوى عمقا داخل غابة قد تزينت بضباب ثمين يمتد لمسافة تبدو كأنها لامتناهية. رونق وسحر هذا الذوق يزداد أريجا بسبب الريح البطيئة والدقيقة والدافئة المنبعثة من خشب الصنوبر الذي يسكن في ضاحية من ضواحي خيالك.

الفن في ذكريات: شد الرحال
Art in Memoirs: Setting Forth

THE HOUSE OF ART AND MEMORIES

Memories are intimately married to art. They nourish one another in subtle ways that are veiled in secret.

Let me paint you a picture of the house where this couple, art and memories, have lived since the beginning of time.

Imagine a meandering path down a forest dressed in an expensive fog that stretches for what seems like an eternity. The luster and magic of the experience is augmented by the slow, meticulous and warm breeze of pine wood lingering in the neighborhood of your imagination.

شكر. إعتاق. فن

الشكر الذي يستحقه الفن هو بسبب السخاء الذي يضحي من خلاله بنفسه في سبيل كل الأرواح المتعطشة. فكلما كانت الأجساد والنفوس مظلومة كلما تلقت نظرة خاصة من منبع الابداع.

ومن خلال عملية إلباس الفقراء بالأنوار والأسرار، يتوجه الفن نحو مثل هذه القلوب المنكسرة على أنها لوحات فارغة وجاهزة للرسم أو كمسرح ينتظر أداء متكامل.

وبعد ذلك، تُحَوّل هذه الموجودات المنكسرة إلى معزوفة تجسد معاني المعاناة التي تجملت بعبيق النصر والمداواة.

الفن في ذكريات: شد الرحال
Art in Memoirs: Setting Forth

GRATITUDE. REDEMPTION. ART

Gratitude is shown towards art for the selflessness through which it grants itself to all thirsty spirits. The more distraught bodies and souls receive a special gaze from the spring of creativity.

In the process of dressing the downtrodden with its lights and secrets, art approaches these broken hearts like empty canvases and a stage awaiting a masterful performance.

Then, art transforms these sundered beings into a symphony of a tragic suffering made beautiful by the fragrance of redemption.

حياة الفنانين القاتلة

الفنان لا يموت أبدا، بل تبقى آثاره طاقة لا تمحى، تحيي عمله الفني في كل لحظة.

فكم هو عجيب هذا الأمر، ترحال الفن. فمن جانب، الحالة الإبداعية تفني جزءا من ذاتك في كل عمل تنتجه.

ومن جانب آخر، ذاك الفناء هو عين خلودك. فتلك البصمة التي يتركها الفنان في نفس المحب هي ذكراه وذكره المقدس.

الفن في ذكريات: شد الرحال

Art in Memoirs: Setting Forth

THE DEADLY LIFE OF ARTISTS

The artist never dies, their traces become an indelible energy constantly bringing their artwork to life.

It is truly a wondrous affair, this journey of art. On the one hand, the creative process annihilates a fraction of your self in every work that is produced.

On the other hand, that annihilation is itself your immortality. The imprint the artist leaves in the loving soul is their memory and remembrance.

على أعتاب البرزخ

جزء من الفنان يجب أن يعيش في غموض، بينما يكمن الجزء الآخر في انضباط، بين الاثنين يستطيع الفنان أن يتسع إلى الفناء في حرفته.

الفن هو الاجتماع المحال بين ماء الحرية العذب وماء الاضطهاد الأجاج، بين الاثنين يظهر الفن كالمستضيف الذي يحرر النهاية من نهايتها ويرزق اللانهاية شيئا من التواضع.

فعلى هذا، الفنان هو مرآة من مرآيّ الفن التي لا نهاية لها. إذا قابلت أحد هذه الانعكاسات، يجب عليك أن تشهد فنه قبل وصول عمله الفني إلى ساحل خيالك، بالضبط كما استطاعت روحه أن تقيم نفسها داخل جسده البسيط المتضائل.

الفن في ذكريات: شد الرحال
Art in Memoirs: Setting Forth

AT THE INTERSTICE

A part of the artist must live in chaos, while the other part lingers in order. Between the two, the artist is able to expand into the nothingness within his craft.

Art is the impossible meeting between the fresh water of liberation and salty water of imprisonment. Between the two, art is the host that liberates finality and humbles infinitude.

The artist, then, is one of the countless mirrors of art. When you meet such a mirror, you should be able to witness their artistry as it arrives at your shore before their artwork, just as their spirit was able to bind itself to their simple body.

على ساحل التعبير

روح الفنان تقهر صنعته تحت الحِرَفية قبل فترة طويلة من وصول الجسد إلى ساحل ذاك التعبير.

ومع هذا، فإن جسد الفنان تأتي إليه ومضات وكشوفات من تلك النهاية والغاية التي قد وصلت إليها روحه.

فيكاد يستطيع الفنان أن يستمع إلى يديه وهما يحركان أوتار آلته الموسيقية بشاعرية نحو الشجن والدموع وملاحظة ريشته وهي ترقص بنفسها نحو وجد ووجدان من الألوان.

الفن في ذكريات: شد الرحال
Art in Memoirs: Setting Forth

AT THE SHORE OF EXPRESSION

The spirit of the artist overwhelms their craft in mastery long before their body is able to reach the shore of that expression.

And yet, during its journey, the body of the artist receives premonitions and beatific visions of the destination which their spirit has reached.

They can almost hear their hands poetically move the strings of their instrument into tears or force the paint brush to dance itself into an ecstasy of colors.

تلاميذ الفرشة والصوت

صحيح! الريشة والأوتار يعيشون في تواضع كامل تحت قوة الفنان. فهما في فناء الحب وفي سبيل الحب.

ولكن هذا أيضا ما هو إلا حجاب يُدهش، بلطف، بعيدا عن أعلى وأرقى أنواع الفناء: ذاك هو زوال الفنان نفسه في أدواته، في تجربة وعمر هذه الأدوات.

فالريشة قد عشقت الألوان بينما يشهد العود حقيقة الصوت. بين هذين يجني الفنان هذه الحقيقة شيئا فشيئا. بعدها، يبدأ يهجر قوته لكي يصبح طالبا عند مدرسة الريشة والعود.

الفن في ذكريات: شد الرحال
Art in Memoirs: Setting Forth

STUDENTS OF BRUSH AND SOUND

It is true, the brush and strings are in complete submission under the power of the artist. They are annihilated in love, for its sake.

But this is also a veil that beautifully distracts from a higher form of annihilation: the fading of the artist within his tools, their experience and age.

The brush is married to colors, and the oud is witnessing sound. The artist gains this realization slowly. Then, they relinquish their power to become students of brush and oud.

جاذبية الفنان

الفنان يمتلك شيء ما يجعلك تتمنى التغيير. ولكن ليس تغييرا فارغا أو مسجونا.

بالعكس، فإن روح الفنان تصقل طريقا يتسلق جبل الصعوبات وصولا إلى قمة الأمل وحلاوة الخلوة.

ذلك لأن الفنان يرتقي بشوقه وحنينه إلى لون أو صوت أو تعبير يعشقه عن بعد. فها هو يتصدق بهدية الشوق والحنين بديهة في أي مكان يتواجد فيه.

الفن في ذكريات: شد الرحال
Art in Memoirs: Setting Forth

THE ARTIST'S ATTRACTION

There is something about the artist that makes you want to change, neither an empty transition nor an imprisoned one.

On the contrary, the artist's spirit chisels a path up the mountain of difficulties to the summit of hope and sweet solitude.

This is because the artist is so sustained by anguish and longing for a beloved color, note and expression in the distance. They involuntarily share this gift wherever they linger.

الموسيقى وخديعة البحار

لقد قال لي يوما أحد الموسيقيين أن علاقة الإنسان ورحلته مع آلته الموسيقية كالغوص في عمق بحر لجي خائن.

فبينما أنت تظن أنك قد وقفت على قدم صدق فوق أعمق خامات اللون الأزرق في قلب هذا البحر، تتحرك أرض الإبداع تحتك لتكتشف الغطاء عن هاوية لا نهاية لها تتكون من ظلال جديدة لهذا اللون.

وهكذا، فبحر الإبداع والفن يبعث لك صديقا في صورة ريشة أو عود ليؤدبك. فيقهرك ومن ثم يشفيك بين تبريح ومداواة ينبعث من جمالهم.

الفن في ذكريات: شد الرحال
Art in Memoirs: Setting Forth

MUSIC AND DECEITFUL OCEANS

I was once told by a musician that one's relationship and journey with their instrument is akin to swimming through a deceitful ocean.

Just when you think you have stood firmly upon the deepest hue of blue, the ground of creativity below you gives way to a bottomless abyss of new shades and tints.

In this way, the ocean of creativity and art sends you a companion in the form of a brush or lute to discipline you. It breaks and heals you between the suffering and redemption of its beauty.

الصدفة والعَجب

للفن أخوين، الصدفة والعَجب. فالفن يطلق سراح فيوضات من النوع الأول عليك حتى يشهدك وأنت تغرق في الثاني.

في المقابل، يجب أن يشهد انعكاس هذين الحركتين في مرآة الفنان. ففيما يخص الاقتباس الحميم للصدفة عند الفنان، فهذا شهوده محاورات لا نهاية لها داخل الألوان والنغمات وبين الألوان والنغمات.

أما فيما يخص عجب ودهشة الفنان، فهو شهوده كل هذه الأحاديث وكأنها نظرة مباركة من الفن. في نهاية الأمر، يظهر أن هذا كله لم يكن إلا حوار باطني قد تم في صمت أزلي.

الفن في ذكريات: شد الرحال
Art in Memoirs: Setting Forth

SERENDIPITY AND WONDER

Art has two siblings, serendipity and wonder. It unleashes upon you floods of the first only in order to observe you drowning in the second.

In return, art likes to witness the reflections of these two movements in the mirror of the artist. The intimate imitation of serendipity to witness endless conversations within colors and notes and between colors and notes.

As for the artist's wonder, it is to witness all these conversations as a gaze of grace from art. In the end, all of this emerges as an inner monologue performed in silence.

في يدي حرفتك

قد لا يكون من الفطنة أن تحسب المقاومة التي تجدها أمامك عند محاولتك الغوص في حرفتك أنها ظلمة لا علاقة لها بالفن.

فللإبداع طرق عجيبة يوصلك من خلالها إلى ساحل الصفاء الفني المطلق. كثير من هذه الطرق تغدو تنتصر ضد عواصف المجهول.

فكما أن الألوان تُظهر نفسها في مرآئي من الاختلافات، والنغمات تتكلم من خلال علاقات محيرة، أنت أيضا عليك أن تجد نفسك في خضم المتضادات.

الفن في ذكريات: شد الرحال
Art in Memoirs: Setting Forth

IN THE HANDS OF YOUR CRAFT

It is perhaps not helpful to assume that the resistance you are facing while attempting to drown in your craft is a darkness external to art.

After all, creativity has wondrous ways in which it delivers you to the shore of pure artistic transcendence. Many of these paths triumph right through a storm of the unknown.

Colors reveal themselves in mirrors of contradictions. Notes and melodies speak through perplexing relationships. And you also, must find yourself amidst the oppositions.

فن الفراق

عليك أن تتعلم كيف تترك وتبتعد، خاصة الابتعاد عن عملك الفني عندما تكمله. دعه يتنفس بنفسه. انظر إليه وكأنه كيان بحد ذاته. دعه يتحدث واترك نفسك تستمع.

فكما أن الريشة ليس لها أن تهنأ نفسها على معزوفة الألوان التي ترمي بها على فضاء اللوحة الفارغة، فأنت أيضا عليك أن تشهد نفسك كالريشة تحركها يد مباركة.

ابحث عن نفسك في خضم كل هذا. ارحل عن عملك الفني ودعه يتنفس. فأنت أيضا قد كنت منحوتا في يوم من الأيام ومن ثم أُبعِدّت حبا لكي تتعلم كيف تشتاق.

الفن في ذكريات: شد الرحال
Art in Memoirs: Setting Forth

THE ART OF LETTING GO

You must learn to let go, especially of your art when it is complete. Let it breathe on its own. Observe it as an entity in its own right. Let it speak and force yourself to listen.

Just as your brush cannot take all the credit for the symphony of colors it unleashes on the empty canvas, also witness yourself as a brush moved by the hand of grace.

Find yourself at the interstice of all of this. Let go of your art and let it breathe. You were also molded once, and distanced in love, so you can learn how to long.

مسكن الفن

بين فنانَين، هنالك نقطة مختفية تلتقي فيها أنفاسهما لتتحد في لازمنية تحمل على ظهرها الكون بأكمله.

بين فنانين، أرواحهما ترعى قصة المعزوفة التي تم إعدادها مسبقا والتي تعتقد أجسادهما أنها تتجلى قِبَل الأنظار.

بين فنانين، الغربة التي ينظر كل منهما من خلالها إلى الآخر تُذكرهم بالهاوية التي يسعون لعبورها متجهين نحو ذواتها، هناك، حيث يكمن الفن.

الفن في ذكريات: شد الرحال
Art in Memoirs: Setting Forth

WHERE ART RESIDES

Between two artists, there is an invisible point where the breaths of their conversations meet and unite into a timelessness that carries the universe.

Between two artists, their spirits oversee the narrative of a choreographed symphony which their bodies believe is unfolding before their gazes.

Between two artists, the separation through which they gaze at one another reminds them of that abyss which they seek to cross towards their essence, where art resides.

في عمق العاصفة

الكمال يوجد في عمق العاصفة. وتمام حرفتك يوجد في الذي يكمن وراءك، في عبث المجهول.

فكل ما ترى أمامك ما هو إلا صورة خامدة كادت أن تمضي وتختفي. وبعدها، عندما تغادر هذه الصورة وتبتعد عن نظرك، يبدو كل ما في الماضي وكأنه حلم.

فانتهي وابدأ من جديد. هذه هي الطريقة الوحيدة التي ستستطيع من خلالها أن تشهد المنبع ونقطة الوصول كأنهما نقطة واحدة من العناق في دائرة الإبداع.

الفن في ذكريات: شد الرحال
Art in Memoirs: Setting Forth

IN THE EYE OF THE STORM

Completion is found in the eye of the storm. The culmination of your craft resides beyond you, in the chaos of the unknown.

All you see in front of you is a lingering metaphor that is coming close to pass. And then, the moment it travels beyond your perception, all that is in the past will seem like a dream.

Finish and begin once again. This is the only way you can witness the origin and destination as a singular point of embrace on the circle of creativity.

عطش الموسيقى

صوت علامة موسيقية واحدة يُوَلّد عطشا لنغمات وإيقاعات قريبة منه. فيكون تاريخه قصة تتجلى من خلال اضطراب الأوتار المجاورة.

هذه العلامات الموسيقية التي تُكَوِّن معزوفة وحيدة ما هي إلا أنفاس في روضة. كل منها له لون وأريج، تعرف نفسها من خلاله في مرآة تعكس أفق كامل من الأنفاس.

فعلى هذا، يا صديقي الفنان، اعلم أن الاستماع إلى العلامات التي تتكلم بها يدك ما هو إلا مكر وسكر: عليك أن تشهد هذا الكلام وكأنه عناق وبعدها انتبه إلى الصمت الذي يكمن بين النغمات.

الفن في ذكريات: شد الرحال
Art in Memoirs: Setting Forth

THE THIRST OF MUSIC

The sound of a single note is born thirsty for nearby melodies and cadences. Its history is narrated through the vibrations of neighboring strings.

These notes of a singular symphony are breaths from a garden. Each with a color and fragrance that knows itself in a mirror reflecting a horizon of these zephyrs.

So know, my artist friend, that listening to the notes which your hand speaks is the ruse of a rose: witness this speech as an embrace and be attentive to the silence between the notes.

شغف الفنان

الفنان لا يبحث عن شيء معين. فذلك ليس ما يتمناه. بل إنه يطلب علاقة وحركة. بخلاف نظرات الآخرين، نظرة الفنان مرتكزة على الحب نفسه.

فالحب هو بعينه حبيب الفنان. كما أن الماء نفسه هو البحر الذي يقطع منه الفنان أعماقا عظيمة، ومن ثم يكسر حاجز العقل عندما يشهد الأزلية بأكملها في قطرة واحدة.

فكلما تموت الحدود، تستطيع أن تجد هنالك انبعاث فنان. ما فهو ينتعش من علاقات تجلب سخرية الموتى، الذين لم يقدروا على الإبحار.

الفن في ذكريات: شد الرحال
Art in Memoirs: Setting Forth

THE DESIRE OF THE ARTIST

The artist seeks not an entity. That is not what they crave. They beseech a relationship and movement. In contrast to other gazes, the artist's are fixed on love itself.

Love is the artist's beloved, just as water itself is the ocean which they traverse to great depths. They break the barrier of reason as they witness eternity in a drop.

Wherever boundaries die, you can find there an artist's resurrection. They thrive on connections that channel mockery from the deceased. Those who cannot sea.

الأصالة بين الأوتار

آلتك الموسيقية تحمل أصالة وثقافة بين حضارة ذراتها الخشبية. أرواح كل المعزوفات التي أدّاها جسد الآلة وغنتها أوتارها تفيض عليها حياة أبدية.

وهذه الروح الحية بين يديك تعرف جيدا أي النغمات تنسجم مع روحك في لحظة معينة. تسرد هذه المسلسلات من الأصوات والإيقاعات تاريخا يومئ إلى مستقبلك.

فعلى هذا، يجب عليك أن تراعي ضوء الشمس والليالي المقمرة في أيام الموسيقى، فهنالك توجد رغبة خاصة في بعض القصص التي لا تؤدى إلا سمعا وفي زي منزه عن الصور.

الفن في ذكريات: شد الرحال
Art in Memoirs: Setting Forth

HERITAGE BETWEEN THE STRINGS

Your instrument carries tradition and culture in-between the empire of its wooden grains. The spirits of all symphonies that have been performed by its body and sung by its strings continue to bring it to life.

This living soul between your hands knows very well which melodies are in harmony with your spirit at any given blink. Altogether, these processions of notes and rhythms inform of a history and foretell your future.

So, be attentive to the sunlight and moonlit nights of music that have peculiar cravings for specific narratives, performed in audition, in a transcendent form.

شعور الفنان الأزلي

يقينا، لا يشعر أحد كالفنان بالذي يحصل خلف ستار الوجود. فإن الذي يتجلى وراء رقصات صور الأجساد هو نفسه الفيض الذاتي للإبداع.

تخيل ساعة رملية تحتضن الأزلية بجميع جلالها ومن ثم ترسلها كذرات من العناق الجميل نحو الأنظار العاشقة.

فكما أن قلب الكون يخسف فيضان الأرواح إلى زي موحد يبعث في الفنان حياة جديدة فالآخر أيضا يصقل وحيا واحدا سرمديا في قصة متواصلة من الأداء الفني.

الفن في ذكريات: شد الرحال
Art in Memoirs: Setting Forth

THE ARTIST'S IMMORTAL FEELINGS

No one feels with conviction what occurs beyond the curtain of existence like the artist. Truly, what transpires behind the dance of bodily forms is itself the unfolding of creativity.

Imagine an hour glass, embracing infinitude in all its majesty and sending it in specks of beautiful embrace towards desiring gazes.

The heart of the universe collapses the deluge of spirits into one dress that brings the artist to life. The artist also molds a single endless inspiration into a narrative of artistic performances.

من التهور إلى الانضباط

قلب الفنان يتفتت تحت تهور الوحي. ما هذا إلا تعذيب متعمد في خضم كل شيء جميل ورؤية منبع الحياة المتذبذب في اتساع لا نهاية له.

ففي بعض الأيام، يجب على الفنان أن يقهر نفسه لكي ينحت جبالا من الإنضباط، في سبيل أن يصل إلى نفخة واحدة من النور تميل غالبا إلى الخمول.

وفي لحظات أخرى، بصر الفنان الثاقب يجد نفسه في وسط أنفاس من النور لا نهاية لها. هنالك يفقد الفنان نظره بحب ورضاء، في سبيل أن يوصل ما هو فان إلى شاطئ السرمدية.

الفن في ذكريات: شد الرحال
Art in Memoirs: Setting Forth

FROM THE AVALANCHE TO ORDER

The artist's heart crumbles under the avalanche of inspiration. It is an intentional torture in all things beautiful, to watch one's vibrating spring of life expand to no end.

Some days, the artist must force himself to chisel through a mountain range of discipline, only to grasp a breath's worth of light which often chooses to hide itself.

Other moments, the artist's focused gaze finds itself amidst countless breaths of light. They are blinded, and love to be so, only to deliver the finite to infinitude.

بين العناق والافتراق

كل أعجوبة تستميل قلب الفنان. فمعبده الباطني ما هو إلا المدينة الفاضلة التي تحوم حولها طرق الزمان عشقا وتتردد عليها دهشة.

في خضم كل هذا يشهد الفنان هذا المهرجان يقينا وعقله مقهورا تحت سلطان التعبير الصادر من المهرجان والذي يقيم بعيدا، وراء شاطئ المنطق.

فإذاً قلب الفنان لوحده له أن يشهد هذه الحركات من الحب المبدع في الآفاق القريبة. في حين تظل روحه في ذوق دائم للمتناقضَين: العناق والافتراق.

الفن في ذكريات: شد الرحال
Art in Memoirs: Setting Forth

BETWEEN EMBRACES AND SEPARATION

Every wonder seeks the artist's heart. Their inner sanctum is the good city around which the paths of time revolve in longing and meander in bedazzlement.

And the artist witnesses this spectacle with conviction while their mind is paralyzed by the expression of its language which lies just beyond the shore of reason.

Only the artist's heart can witness these motions of creative love in the nearby horizons. Meanwhile, their spirit remains constantly tasting, both union and separation.

على خطى الأولياء

على خطى الأولياء، يلحظ الفنان عالمه ويؤثر فيه من خلال أنظاره. فكل ما أصدر خياله من سحر يُترجم إلى ازدهار ولمعان ظاهرين.

هذا لأن الفنان يعلم أن كل ما يوجد في الخارج ينبسط باطنا. فعمله الفني الذي يجسد بحره الباطني يكشف الستار أيضا عن روح الكون.

ومع هذا، فالفنان أيضا يتقن فن التحولات. فهو في انسجام تام مع نغمة الحركة التي تتحكم بوشم الإغراء الذي تتجلى نغماته فوق قمة الوجود، ذلك القصيد الذي أصم العقل.

الفن في ذكريات: شد الرحال
Art in Memoirs: Setting Forth

UPON THE FOOTSTEPS OF SAINTS

Like saints, artists perceive their world and cause change in it through their gazes. Whatever their imagination conjures of glamour, it translates into our precious glitter.

This is because the artist knows that whatever exists without is unfolding within. Their work, which externalizes their inner ocean, also reveals the spirit of the universe.

And yet, artists are also masters of transition. They are in tune with the tone of movement governing the siren song at the cosmic summit; that hymn which deafens reason.

همسات الصوت

استمعت لفترة يبدو وكأنها أبدية. أنصت إلى همسات صوتي داخل تذبذبات هواجسي الفنية.

رأيت بعين البصيرة الصور التي تولدت من تلك الهمسات. شاهدت أقدارها تتجلى من عذاب الفراق وهي تغادر بعيدا عن الأنظار.

قيل لي في تلك اللحظة أن الإبداع مقابلة وعناق أزلي بين الفراق واللقاء، زفير وشهيق تلاشوا في هاوية من الزمن.

الفن في ذكريات: شد الرحال
Art in Memoirs: Setting Forth

THE WHISPERS OF SOUND

I listened for what seemed like an eternity. I even heard the whispers of my own voice within the reverberations of my artistic inclinations.

I foresaw the forms which these whispers gave birth to. I even witnessed their destinies emanating from their agonies of separation as they depart beyond sight.

I was told, at that moment, that creativity is a meeting and eternal embrace between departure and arrival. An exhalation and inhalation collapsed in time.

قناع شهوات الروح

تحت أي قناع تأمل أن تقمع شهوات الروح وتردها عن شوقها نحو البحر والساحل، باطنا بين اللؤلؤة وضيائها؟

هل تحدّث معك شخص ما عن سر يكاد يمحيك من الوجود لو تفوهت به أو يموت مع جسدك إذا سترته؟ ألم تشعر بعناقه الرحيم ومع هذا ما زلت تشك بصدق أريجه؟

هذه شذرات تقهر الشمس تواضعا وجلالا. بعضنا لا يرى سوى قتالا بين أضواء هذه الملحمة، بينما ترى الشمس حرقة إبداعية قد فاقت موتها وشوقها.

الفن في ذكريات: شد الرحال
Art in Memoirs: Setting Forth

THE MASK OF THE SPIRIT'S DESIRE

Under what disguise do you hope to rend the cravings of your spirit from the longing it has towards the ocean and shore, inwardly between the pearl and its luster?

Did someone speak to you of a secret that will dissipate you if uttered or will die with your body otherwise? Have you felt its merciful embrace yet still distrust its fragrance?

These are fragments that shun the sun through their glory. Some of us only see a clash of lights in this epic, but the sun sees a creative burn that surpasses its own demise.

لوحة فارغة وريشة غامضة

تحت ظل شجرة كريمة تنمو بذرة العجائب التي تغذي إبداع الفنان. كإعصار من الأريج العبق، تملأ هذه العجائب نسيج وضياء الفضاء.

هذا بينما يحتضن الفنان دفء الحب تحت ظل الشجرة. إن هذه حادثة عظيمة، تتجلى فيها حرقة العناق من خلال الظلال.

في مكان آخر، بعيدا عن أفق الشجرة، هنالك لوحة فارغة تُجَسّد لمسة رسامها الخالد، لمسة تظهر بريشة غامضة وألوان هادئة.

الفن في ذكريات: شد الرحال
Art in Memoirs: Setting Forth

AN EMPTY CANVAS, UNKNOWN BRUSH

Under the shade of a magnanimous tree grows the seed of wonders that nurtures the artist's creativity. Like a typhoon of fragrance, it fills the texture and glow of the ambiance.

Meanwhile, the artist is embracing the warmth of love under the shade of the tree. This is one auspicious occasion, where a searing union is felt through shadows.

Somewhere, beyond the horizon of the tree, there is an empty canvas that is reproducing the touch of its immortal painter, with an invisible brush and serene shades.

الشعور بجمال الضنك

الفنان يحمل على كتفيه جبل الأقدار، ويخطو خطوات مرموقة نحو انسجام سماوي، ويتلألأ بحياة خافتة من بعد.

الفنان يشعر أيضا بجمال الضنك الذي قد صار مبهما عند باقي الكهنة والقسايسة. يشهد الفنان روحه وهي ترتجل في أرجاء صوت ولون قد اختفيا عن جسده وعقله.

هذا الفرق، بين الجسد والروح، يفتت الفنان إلى تجريد من الحب. ولا يزال يندمج مع حرفته حتى يصبح أريج خافت من الدهشة والذكريات.

الفن في ذكريات: شد الرحال
Art in Memoirs: Setting Forth

SENSING THE BEAUTY OF MISERY

The artist carries the mountain of fate upon their shoulders, solemnly marching towards a heavenly equilibrium, barely glowing with life in the distance.

The artist feels a beauty of suffering made oblivious to other seers and monks. They witness their spirits basking in a sound and color to which their bodies are made blind.

This separation, between body and spirit, disintegrates the artist into an abstraction of love. They continue to melt with their craft, until they become a faint breeze of wonder and memory.

جوهرة تتصبب عرقا

هل رأيت مرة جوهرة تتصبب عرقا يتكون من سجلات الحب ويتواجد في أنحاء آفاقها؟ كأنها تتلألأ بأعاجيب تجذب آذان المستمعين المضطهدين عشقا.

هكذا يكون قلب الفنان ومقامه في أفلاك الإلهام الروحية. بدورها، أهدت زينة الإبداع هذه أشباحا مَجازية ملأت عالم الصور.

ولكنها لم تعطنا هذه الأنفاس الراقية من الزجاج لكي نتناسى أنا وأنت، ولكن لنتذكر دائمًا ذاك القلب الأصيل، الذي تكمن ذكراه خلف ستار الذكريات.

الفن في ذكريات: شد الرحال
Art in Memoirs: Setting Forth

THE PRESPIRATING JEWEL

Have you ever seen a jewel that perspires tomes of love within the proximity of its own horizons? It glows with wonders that attract anguished listeners.

That is the heart of the artist and his status in the spiritual spheres of inspiration. As a gift, this hidden ornament of creativity gave forth metaphors that fill the world of forms.

It did not simply give us these breezes of elegant glass for you and me to forget, but to remember incessantly that original heart. A remembrance beyond memory.

يا حضرة الفنان

الإلهام الإبداعي يصل إلى حضرة الفنان كفيضان من الفجر وشموس ساطعة من الصدف الكريمة. واحدة تلو الأخرى، تُحَوّل هذا الإعصار من ومضات مفترقة إلى نظرة لا نهاية لها.

هذا الفجر وهيبته العذرية التي تعرف بالليل الهادئ تحيط بالفنان كإبتهالات تأتي من بعيد. تتحاور مع القلب وتطيح بالعقل من عرشه ومسؤوليته.

وبعد هذا يبدأ هؤلاء الزائرون بالرحيل شيئا فشيئا ويتركون خلفهم آثارا محرقة من الشوق تخلف ورائها فقط شيئا بسيطا من الصبر يكفي لإنتظار الفجر القادم، يكون شروقا جديدا من الألوان ولكن في لمحة مألوفة.

الفن في ذكريات: شد الرحال
Art in Memoirs: Setting Forth

DEAR MR. ARTIST

Creative inspiration arrives into the presence of the artist like a flood of dawns and rising suns of serendipity. One after the other, this deluge transforms blinks into an endless gaze.

The dawn, and its virginal anticipation known as the tranquil darkness, envelop the artist like chants from a distance. They converse with the heart and absolve reason of responsibility.

And then, these subtle visitors depart, leaving behind them burning traces of longing that grant just enough patience to await the coming dawn, a new break of colors in a similar glance.

استفسار فني

أخبرني، كم من فترة أخرى تودني أن أعاني وأنا أتربص يدك الجليلة التي تتردد بين ومضات من الألوان وتحولات من النغمات؟

إلى أي أفق ترسلني بهمسات أنفاسك هذه التي تتحدث صمتا عن أرض من العجائب نائمة بعيدا داخل سرك؟

هل هو الصبر الجميل الذي تريده أن يرتسم بالألم في قلبي؟ أم أنه رحيلك أنت عن آداب الرحمة المتداولة بين الفنانين، نحو مكائد السماء وجنانها؟

الفن في ذكريات: شد الرحال
Art in Memoirs: Setting Forth

AN ARTISTIC INQUIRY

Tell me, how much longer do you wish me to suffer in anticipation of your glorious hand that hesitates between blinks of colors and cadences of notes?

To what horizon are you sending me with the whispers of your breaths that speak in silence of a land of wonders slumbering far away, within your secret?

Is it sweet patience that you painfully desire to imprint upon my heart? Or is it your own departure from the etiquette of mercy known among artists, towards the ruse of heavens?

تشدق نغمات الإبداع

هنالك لحظات تتشدق فيها نغمات الإبداع حولك كأنها آثار عطرة من الهواء أو صفحات تاريخية من قصة الضوء. كلاهما يرتحل ويعطيك دهشة.

هذه هي اللحظات التي تتيقن من خلالها أن أبواب الزيارة السماوية قد فتحت أيديها لك. وأن هنالك نظرة خاصة من ذات الفن متجهة نحوك، بعيدا عن كل شيء آخر.

فلا تحاول أن تصطنع عناية زائفة لإتحاف مثل هذه اللحظات. فقط استمع إلى النسمات والضياء وهم يملؤون وجدانك قصصا ستحتاج إليها لكي تستمر في رحلتك.

الفن في ذكريات: شد الرحال
Art in Memoirs: Setting Forth

MELODIES OF DECLAMATION

There are moments when the notes of inspiration flow around you like fragrant traces of air or pages of history from the story of light. They wander and give wonder.

These are the moments when you know that the gates of visitation have opened their arms for you. There is a special gaze from Art itself towards you and away from all else.

Do not attempt to exert artificial effort to show these moments your care. Simply listen to the breezes and glow as they fill your being with the stories needed for you to continue your journey.

لا تغادر أرض الفن

حتى تواني الفنان يعتبر إبداعا. وقدرته على الرحيل بعيدا عن ملمس اليدين يُوَلّد ضياء خاصا في مثل هذه اللحظات من الراحة المصطنعة.

كلا، إنه ليس التواني في إنتاج فنا ملموسا الذي عليك أن تخشاه من الفنان، بل ما يُخاف عليه هو مغادرته أرض الفن والتنازل عن زي التجديد.

بل يجب على الفنان أن يتوانى بعض الشيء لكي يسمح لأمانيه الزائفة بأن ترتحل إلى الصدق عن طريق أرض الخيال، بينما يأخذ هو هذه الأماني بيديه، من الوهم إلى شهود الجماح.

الفن في ذكريات: شد الرحال
Art in Memoirs: Setting Forth

DON'T DEPART FROM THE LAND OF ART

Even the artist's procrastination is creative. Their ability to venture beyond the grasp of hands and touch is born with a special glow during such moments of artificial comfort.

No, it is not procrastination in producing tangible art that you should fear for the artist, but their departure from the presence of art and relinquishing the garb of novelty.

The artist must procrastinate in order to allow his false hopes to journey to truth through the land of imagination. He takes them by the hand, from whim to witnessed fantasy.

حوار السوق

بينما هو واقف يشتري بعض الأشياء من المحل البارحة، رأى الفنان شخصا من وطنه العتيق. وسمع اللغة الأم على لسانه، ومن ثم شاهد تعبيراته ورأى ماضيه كله في عينيه.

وما جعل الأمور أكثر حيرة هو أن الرجل الغامض لم يعتنق حديثا عميقا مع صديقه بل طلب منه بعض النقود وحسب. ومع هذا، فهو قد زين كلامه بقدر يكفي من التاريخ.

فجأة، تحولت ألوان الجدران والرفوف في المحل إلى بيت سحري يكمن في خيال مفقود. عندها، عثر الفنان على إلهامه الجديد.

الفن في ذكريات: شد الرحال
Art in Memoirs: Setting Forth

A CONVERSATION AT THE MARKETPLACE

Standing in line at the marketplace yesterday, an artist saw a man from back home. He heard his own native language on the other's tongue. He witnessed his expressions and saw his entire past in his eyes.

To make matters more elusive, the man did not have a deep conversation with his friend, but merely asked for money. And yet, he ornamented his speech with just enough history.

Suddenly, the colors of the walls of the marketplace and the racks transformed into an enchanted home residing in lost imagination. The artist found his next inspiration.

مسكن العقل والمنطق

"هل تعلم أين مسكن العقل والمنطق؟" سألت الهواء حولي مرة. فأجابني بكامل وجدانه: "تَوّني عدت من حضرته الآن، ففي الحقيقة أنا هنا وهناك."

"كيف يمكن ذلك؟"، استعجبت من الهواء. فأجاب بجلال: "ألا تشعر بالحركة تستيقظ داخلي؟" وافقته وقلت: "نعم، أراها تسري من لا مكان إلى الذي بيننا."

فأجاب الهواء: "إذا اعلم أن العقل يعيش تحت جسر كوني، يحمل على كتفيه عرش الفن. الملك هناك يتحدث مع القلب ومن ثم يفضي مطرا يتجلى على الفقراء الذي يقيمون أسفل منه."

الفن في ذكريات: شد الرحال
Art in Memoirs: Setting Forth

THE ABODE OF INTELLECT AND LOGIC

"Do you know where reason resides?" I asked the air around me once. It replied with the entirety of its being: "I just came back from its presence, I am actually there and here!"

"How can that be?", I wondered. The air replied majestically: "Do you not feel movement escalating within me?" I concurred: "Yes, it is flowing from nowhere to between us!"

The air replied: "Then know that reason lives under a cosmic bridge that supports the throne of art. The king converses with the heart and filters rain that descends upon the poor ones below."

لغة أقدم من الزمن

هنالك عروج للرياح يظهر لك حين تتأمل أجساد الحروف ورسمها القديم، يصل إليك المعنى من خلالها في صمت تام.

هنالك لغة، أقدم من الزمن وتشتاق إلى هذا التراث الجمالي من الصورة والعبيق. يتحدث بها لسان القلب من خلال أثير الصوت العتيق.

فإذاً التمس جانبك الفني بواسطة ذات قلبك لإن هذه اللغة قد أقفلت أبوابها أمام العقل وموسمه. ولكن اعلم أن في نفس الوقت هذا الإغلاق هو عناق للفنان لا نهاية له.

الفن في ذكريات: شد الرحال

Art in Memoirs: Setting Forth

A LANGUAGE OLDER THAN TIME

There are meandering breezes that appear as you contemplate the bodies of letters and their ancient calligraphy. Meaning is conveyed to you in silence.

There is a language, older than time itself, that hearkens to such aesthetic traditions of form and fragrance. This tongue of the heart speaks through primordial sound.

So touch your artistic side with the essence of your heart. For this language has closed its gates for reason and its season. Yet, its closure is an unbounded embrace for the artist.

غذاء من الفراق

الفراق هو غذاء الفنان. البعد عن كل معنى، حتى نفسك، بل هو الشوق الذي يعطي الفنان القوة للخوض في ما لا نهاية له.

والماضي ليس فقط بُعد زمني، بل مكاني أيضا. تأمل أطلال سطوح وملموسات معشوقة تظهر الآن من هاوية الزمن. هل تغريك لزيارتها مجددا؟

لنفترض أنها ما زالت موجودة في أشباحها الهيكلية، ما الذي يتبقى من أرواحها الأصلية التي كانت تملأ أثير المكان؟ أهي التي تغيرت أم أن روحك تجتاح أفاق الشيخوخة بسرعة أكبر؟

الفن في ذكريات: شد الرحال
Art in Memoirs: Setting Forth

THE SUSTENANCE OF SEPARATION

Separation is the sustenance of the artist. Distance from all things and meanings, even oneself, is the longing that grants the artist power to embrace infinitude.

The past is not only distance in time, but in place as well. Reminisce over the traces of beloved textures from the abyss of time. Do you crave revisiting them?

Assume they still exist in their skeletal effigies, what remnants of their original spirits still linger in the vicinity? Did they change or is your spirit aging faster than them?

الفن في ذكريات: شد الرحال
Art in Memoirs: Setting Forth

www.ingramcontent.com/pod-product-compliance
Lightning Source LLC
Chambersburg PA
CBHW021444210526
45463CB00002B/631